wheatfields
& vineyards

RALPH W. SEAGER

Christian Herald House
40 Overlook Drive, Chappaqua, New York 10514

Grateful acknowledgement is made to the following:
Christian Living for permission to reprint PERPETUAL CARE
The Kansas City Star for permission to reprint APPLE TREES GROW FOR
WINTER, FIELD-STONE FENCE, WILD FIRE, TOUCH OF WILDNESS,
WINTER MILKING, WILD MYSTERY, A BARN IS A MIRACLE, SHAPE OF A
RING, SAD ARE THE HORNS, THE RIDER, MEMORY: HAVING AT ONE'S
FINGER TIPS
The Link for permission to reprint AN OCCASIONALLY FOGGY DAY
McCall's for permission to reprint THAT CATCH OF BREATH
New Hampshire Profiles for permission to reprint PUMP HANDLE and
THE SIBILANT DRUMS
Oregonian for permission to reprint DANDELIONS
Poetry View for permission to reprint FEATHER PILLOW
Purpose for permission to reprint INTO THE MORNING
The Rhode Islander for permission to reprint BAGGAGE ALLOWANCE and
ONE WAY A BLACKBIRD LOOKED AT ME
Today for permission to reprint REACH TO THE ROSE
Wake-Brook House for several poems, copyright by Ralph W. Seager

DEDICATION

*To all my students who made clear to me what the
ancients have known since Galatians:*

> *When anyone is under instruction . . .
> he should give his teacher a share of all
> good things he has.   (Gal. 6:6)*

*This they have done to my everlasting gratitude and
Love, and it is to each of them this book is dedicated.*

the land

the people

wheatfields
& vineyards

THE COUNTRY ROAD on which I was walking
lipped over the brim of the Pinnacle, then took off on
a headlong dash to wet its dusty tongue in the clear
blue lake below. I let it go for the moment and turned
my face to the breeze to cool the fever fired by the long,
hot climb. The road was accompanied by random dai-
sies, buttercups, and cornflowers. It was a good place to
stop. Standing there on this high tide of geology, I
looked down upon the spine of Bluff Point.

Bluff Point is, in a sense, a sort of inland peninsula
which separates the "Y" branches of Keuka Lake. My
eyes roamed over the scene beneath me, centering on
the miniature farms, their red barns, and white, green-
shuttered houses. I saw this farmscape as a plaidwork
of cloth, patterned by the stitch and cross-stitch of
fences.

Then into my delight crept the awareness of a recur-
rent theme. These plaids were wheatfields and vineyards keeping good company together. Wheat and
grapes: Bread and Wine. This was not the thin wafer,
but the loaf—sun-crusted and sweet with wheat. Here
was not the sip, but the purpled goblet. There was no
elaborately scrolled table, only the good earth upon

which this cloth was spread. But there was bread by the ovensful, wine by the cask. And not a deacon, not a vestryman in sight. It was Communion by the acre!

These Bluff Point farmers, these harvesters of wheat and tenders of grapevines, know that before the wheat is flour there must be tilling and planting, harvesting and threshing. The farmer, like his wheat, knows something of the millstone's grinding. So it is with the vineyardist: he, too, knows that before the grape is wine there must be setting and post driving, trimming and tying. He, like his grapes, knows something of the screw of the winepress. He is at it season through season; his remembrance is day-by-day—everyday. Communion, in his life, is more than a special occasion. It is the livelihood of life. Surely, I thought as I strode down the road, this must be pleasing to Him.

Farmers and the good earth, grape growers and good roots extend the mutual handclasp of primal communion between those who live on the land and the land of the living. Both man and earth are God given. From barn to meadow, valley to mountain, brookside to lakeside, the countryside is God's own witness to His goodwill toward His children.

So I have brought these poems together in a kind of communion—bread for the hungers of life—wine for the thirsts. All readers are welcome to taste.

—Ralph W. Seager

the land

WHEAT AND GRAPES

Bluff Point farmers sow their wheat
Close against their Concord vines,
Where purple goblets hold the wines
That rain and sunshine pour so sweet.

Bluff Point farmers see it right—
That wheat and vineyards should unite,
Since bread and wine fulfill this union
In the serving of Communion.

A BARN IS A MIRACLE

Here is a miracle painted red,
A weathervane upon its head
With sliding panels in the walls,
The hidden doors and secret stalls.

The wheat upon this threshing floor
Once stood in acres, score on score;
And all of June stacked in this pile
Was hay and clover by the mile.

With summer high up in the mows
Above the sheep, above the cows,
The small teeth nibbling in the bin—
So winter's barn takes all things in.

Here, in this small and magic box,
The farmer crowds his fields and flocks;
Arithmetic can never tell
How one barn holds the farm so well.

FIELD-STONE FENCE

His field lay clogged, and long before
His plow could stir the sunlight in
He had to stack the scattered store
Of rocks that wore this acre thin.

He built this fence of quiet peace,
Which never fortified the land,
Or said the neighbor's world must cease
Exactly where these riftrocks stand.

Now chipmunks flick along its shelves
Where mosses hush the splintered stones,
And hermit thrushes dare themselves
To try their treble, double-tones.

No barrier in length or height,
But a resting place when feet may falter,
These field-stones built a fence all right,
I think they almost raised an altar.

OWED TO A COUNTRY ROAD

My old roads now are black-top and concrete;
I cannot feel the country through my feet,
Or know its shadowed breeze upon my skin,
Remembering where woods once crowded in
To watch with green eyes what was going by;
Now all that's left is road—and open sky.
I miss the quiet, cool, receptive clay
That caught my print, springing me on the way;
The dust beams walking up the slanting stair
As leaves slid down the banister of air.
Bulldozers gouge and steel blades cut straight through,
No sudden turns—no unexpected view
Of doe and fawn, or Paisley pheasant's brood
To grace and color rural solitude.
I see my hills knocked down, my valleys spanned
Where roads once fitted kindly to the land.

THE FOSTER HEART

Old folks said this twisted tree
From the first was devil-cursed.
All its branches writhed and groaned,
It stood defeated and disowned,
Just as though a baneful oath
Had been sworn against its growth,
For years of struggle in the earth
Had not brought one bud to birth.

Then two kissed here and said this tree
Of all the rest was heaven-blessed.
And so they carved their Cupid's mark
With both initials in the bark.
And in that April's secret air,
The tree swelled big and blossomed fair,
Till summer filled its fruitful part . . .
All it needed was a heart.

SMALL BELLS WALKING

Down from the meadows the small bells are talking.
I have not heard them since I was a child;
Here I will linger to see the cows walking
Out of the sunset, full-uddered and mild.

Bells and sweet clover, and watch-winding crickets,
Jerseys and Guernseys with ripe plums for eyes;
Square chimes now ringing the chapels in thickets,
Bring back the days that were lovely—and wise.

I have heard bells in the thundering tower,
Clangorous steeple, the vast muffled dome;
Heart is my ear in this evening hour,
Hearing small carols on cows coming home.

BOVINE BALLET

This cow came lumbering down the lane,
Hip-joint-heavy, her udder heaving;
Of all God's creatures on hill or plain
How this one goes is past believing.

Bound and burdened with bone and milk,
I wonder she ever moves quicker than walking;
Yet some of her movements are fluid as silk,
And I witnessed one that ceased all my mocking.

A sweatfly fastened itself to her cheek
And left the bite of his small torch a-burning.
She stopped—her neck became supple and sleek,
Bending around in an elegant turning.

She stood in a circle, her hoof to her face,
And there by the touch of a delicate reaching
Fingered the itch with incredible grace,
While I stood astonished to study such teaching.

FEATHER PILLOW

I watched this duck ride in on river-tide,
Rise to the shore in awkward, straddling stride;
His red-webbed paddles that ruddered every turn
Moved clumsily, and set too far astern.
He could not bring his natural ease to shore;
He wanted buoyancy of water more
Than sand and gravel slope, or so I thought.
But then he made a marvelous move and taught
Me how that jewelled swivel let him spin
His neck from north to south. I'll never win
That trick—my bones, ill-fashioned for such grace
Envy his sleeping backwards with his face.

TOUCH OF WILDNESS

When I called to that chickadee
By whistles he could understand,
He left his wild wings in the tree
And came on tame ones to my hand.

There in one quick flight he spanned
My world of domesticity;
Or could it be that he had scanned
The touch of wildness still in me?

WILD MYSTERY

Although he tries as best he can,
Some things are far too strange for man.

There is a time that I remember
From the white days of December,

When I saw that crippled deer
Come down the trail. He passed so near

That I could see the shattered peg
Some hunter left him for a leg.

Yet brighter wonders on that trail
Came with a limping cottontail

Who also knew how a bullet struck,
And he stayed close beside that buck.

I watched these wounded, wild hearts go
On tethered tracks across the snow,

Till two white tails had left with me
Their strange, and holy, mystery.

THREAD OF HUNGER

The high hawk hangs on the thread of hunger,
Swinging tautly from the sky;
The scimitar is in his talon,
Need is burning through the eye.

And there are wings above all creatures,
Lending pinions to the fate
That drops in swift and silent mercy . . .
Hunger has no time for hate.

THE SHOT

It was a cider-mellow morning
    Where I stood.
The air was pipe-smoke-grey
Where beeches puffed among the cedars.
I was tasting the apple-crack of sweetness;
And the gun lay light along my elbow.
    Up from my feet
The grouse thundered
On spiral lightning.
I put out his fire—and more—
As a red leaf, snicked by a pellet, fell,
Mortally wounding Summer.

WILD FIRE

He raced on charcoal legs across the snows,
A plume of fire with pencil-pointed nose,
A puff of white smoke at his bushy tail,
The only burning thing in winter's trail.

He left the field and scorched the upper rail
Of an old split fence, and my rifle quickly rose
And caught him in the sights. He stopped to pose,
And all his fiery beauty glowed so bright
I would not quench the flame I could not light.

SWAMP-FIRE

The dark swamp shivers with the wind,
And I, as downcast as the sky,
Hurry on with wintry heart
In hopes my cabin will be dry.

The marsh reeds rattle in the gale,
The ice-bound bay curls up its lip,
Baring its white teeth at my heels,
And growls because I flee its grip.

No cheering vision in this place,
No lifting hope that men require,
Until two cardinals flash ahead
And set the swamp and me a fire.

ONE WAY A BLACKBIRD LOOKED AT ME

The crow rose
Straight up
From the snow ditch.
His cape sleeves,
Frayed by
A loose stitch,
Snagged on a tree
He thought to clear.
There he perched
Broom-sticked,
Like a night witch
Faustus hood
Drawn to mantled shoulder.
He, that white day,
Laid such caw-curse
Upon me
That for
Two fields after
I saw naught but
BLACK.

SIGHT UNSEEN

Whose eyes were watching I do not know,
I'd come for berries with my wooden pail;
The land was wilder; it was years ago
Since I had wandered this far off the trail.

No bluejay called, and they are first to tell
When anything has come within a mile;
No silent deer stepped out, yet I know well
That there were eyes upon me all the while.

Although the pail showed less than half a peck,
I thrashed my way out through the brambled screen.
There's something in the spine and nape of neck
That does not like the feel of sight unseen.

INTO THE MORNING

Into the morning a small bird came winging
Up to the cherry bough whitening my door.
Out of his flute-throat his wild pulse was flinging
Notes he had learned from an unwritten score.

Roused from my sleep, I turned on my pillow
Away from the shadow belonging to night,
Watching the bird ride the blossoming billow
As breezes kept rolling him into my sight.

If in the dark there is kept for our keeping
A lark or a longspur to bring in the dawn,
So may it be in a far longer sleeping
There'll be a small bird to wake us with song.

LOST GRAVEYARD

It's strange that death no longer turns his eye
To where he stopped so often in the past,
Yet not in eighty years has he come by
To write a newer slate beside the last.

Old headstones tire of holding up the years,
Their names are resting well, they will abide them.
And none will care, since there are no more tears,
If stones let go and lie down there beside them.

FIRST CLAIM

He always liked sweet peas along his shack,
Where summer warmed him and his weathered chair.
He sat a-tilt in rainbows at his back,
His single wish was that the day be fair.

Yet autumn came, and all his days were done.
Then I went by to put his chair away,
Only to find that his sweet peas had run
Their green arms fast around . . . I let it stay.

ROSES ON AN OLD HOUSE

The house had stumbled to its knees,
The cellar door leaned off askew;
One window still held light in it
But all the rest let darkness through.

The grass grew hay-high at the porch
Where wooden steps had tripped and fallen,
Yet roses . . . roses over all,
And bees a-dusting in the pollen.

No hands are there to nail and paint,
And no quick shears to trim severely;
Small wonder—now I think of it,
Why roses mend that house so dearly.

PERPETUAL CARE

It must have been a hundred years ago
The house burned down. There's nothing left to show
Except the chimney-headstone marks the grave,
Sunken into the cellar. Grass forgave
The flame and buried what the fire consumed.
No telling now where life herein was roomed,
Where bed, and parlor, kitchen, shed, once was.
Or if this homestead heard small children buzz
Around and bring their sweets into the hive.
Yet one thing's sure, it once was all alive.
Now daffodils tie down the greening mat
And as for wreaths—wild roses see to that.

THE WILD TAKES OVER WHEN
THE TAME GIVES UP

It happens when the mailbox has no name,
The farmer's gone, his sons have gone the same.
It's then the wild takes over when the tame
Gives up. I've seen the pines leave home and step
Across the fence to be with apple trees,
Abandoned, tired, and bent upon their knees.
I've seen the partridge pinwheel from the cedars
And roost upon the ridgepole of the shed,
The doe and stag with high head antler-tossed
Take over salt licks that the sheep have lost.
The fox moves in to dig where fields were plowed;
He likes the earth that has been stirred before.
The owl drifts closer in on grey wool wings;
The night is dominoed with fire-eyed things.
It's true the wild are always pressing in;
The chance of man's default is theirs to win.
And so the wild grape twines the vineyard posts;
Wild cherries walk with sweet ones turned to ghosts.
Even where man offends to hold his line
The wild comes back compassionate, benign,
Leaning forever on the fence and road
Embracing the mound where is our last abode.

BAGGAGE ALLOWANCE

I have, on snowshoes,
walked over fence posts
and small Christmas trees.
   I have savored new
   potatoes and green
   peas floating in a
   dairy of hot milk
   and melted butter.
I have heard the thrush
singing double tones
through two flutes at once.
   I have smelled cider-
   wine in the summer
   harvest apple tree.
I have seen autumn
strike its match and make
sparklers of poplars.
   These I shall declare
   as allowed baggage
   when my Flight departs,
But the things I've felt
I shall smuggle in
undeclared: the heart's
excess carry-ons.

PROTECT ME NOT

My policy states that I am covered
From loss by various acts of God:
Tornadoes, hail, and flooding waters
In terms more limited than broad.

Whereas, consideration of
premiums paid in full when due,
still we cannot compensate,
to wit, the following risks to you:

The act of arson in the fall
when ivy sets fire to your wall—

nor shady deals and other gyps
when the sun goes in eclipse—

the daisy's petalled-perjury
who swore to tell the truth for free—

nor the moon's unprovable alibi
when shadows steal before the eye.

I've read the fine print on the page,
And though I forfeit future wage,
I waive all claims against such fraud;
Protect me not from these acts of God.

AN OCCASIONAL FOGGY DAY

I like an occasional foggy day.
It softens the edges of the bay
Where boats loom up as out of dreams,
And nothing is quite what it seems.
What was lovely in the light,
Takes on the shape of fear and fright,
And what was ugly in the sun,
Is now—the most handsomely done.
From under this greying, floating shawl
Peer faces I cannot recall,
Yet, still and all we walk together,
Spirits in this gentle weather.
Fog so full it hides the steeple
Cannot blot the form of people.
Yes, though a child of light, I say
I like an occasional foggy day.

DANDELIONS

Father-Sun shone warm on Mother-Green
and in the Spring
A thousand sons,
Ten thousand little suns were seen.

NOTHING IS LOST

Autumn's last spectra show first in the Springtime,
Willows come gold before they turn green,
October's red fills the cane of the berry
Standing knee-deep in the snowdrift's last scene.

Nothing is lost from the time of the harvest,
Trees drip their colorings into earth's wells,
Till March, with its small pumps eternally dipping,
Primes this new life-blood before the green tells.

Indian Summer has saved its last yellow
To flower forsythia, fronting its leaf;
So shall we turn in the all-cycling orbit,
Nothing is lost and there's no need for grief.

APPLE TREES GROW FOR WINTER

Apple-tree wood burns well in the winter,
July and August are fast in its grain;
And a slab on the hearth or a chunk in the heater
Is summer let free in a whiter domain.

Cortlands and Baldwins flavor December,
The colder the weather, the better the pie!
In the dark of the cellar—a barrel of cider,
And hot mugs around when New Year comes by.

There's something that's right about winter and apples,
From cords of split sunshine to Spies on a tray.
Is it then any wonder, when blossoms are falling
That an apple tree orchard makes snow storms in May?

THAT CATCH OF BREATH

Now Autumn pulls the shawl around its shoulder
And rocks a little faster on the porch;
The apples in the paring pan are colder,
The sugar maple flares into a torch.
The corn shocks turn to wigwams in the valleys,
Indian Summer lights its signal smokes,
While pumpkins strew the fields for harvest rallies,
The sun rubs off its burnish on the oaks.
Where bittersweet festoons the rural fences,
Our elemental rue drinks its own tear;
The green and gold that growing, joyed our senses,
Bleeds red into the heartbreak of the year.
   There is in everything that gives us gladness
   That catch of breath that touches us with sadness.

THE WINDS OF MARCH

The winds of March wind up the willow trees
All through the day, until their springs are tight;
Taunting the boughs, they run off with the keys,
Leaving the trees to unwind through the night.

They vex the crow, stalling him in the air;
Laugh in his face, watching his black wings flail
In losing fight against their whistling dare,
Then, when he turns, give him a pigeon's tail.

Impudent as these winds of March may be,
Seldom with warmth, most often sharp and thin,
I've seen them move a winter leaf and free
A crocus bloom, to let a numbed bee in.

THE SIBILANT DRUMS

It's a silent path that glides toward the town,
Edging the slope where Jonathan tends his squash.
And clean swept too—not so much as a twig
To snap the silence. No tree, small or big,
Stands along its way and freshets wash
The long, soft grass smoothly combing it down.

But nearer town, dividing a colonnade
Of maples, lined straight as a spoke from rim
To village hub, the path lies ankle-deep
In frost-dried leaves since none lives by to sweep
Them clear. And there the sibilant drums for him
Are played, whose footsteps march his own parade.

SAD ARE THE HORNS

Sad are the horns that sound in October,
Sadly they blow for the youth of the year;
For the young dreams that slept too late into springtime,
For the loves that were lost when summer walked here.

Sad for the egg that never was broken,
The robin's round grave when he should have been free.
Sad for the apple that ripened ungathered,
The best one of all, but too high in the tree.

So the months go and fall, like a father,
Takes up these children to his kind knee;
Sad are the horns that sound in October
For the dreams and the loves that never shall be.

WILD HEAVEN

When I catch my second breath
And run again the other side of death,
If there's a choice then I'll request
The heaven that will suit me best.

No marble halls or streets of gold,
No harps to play or angel-wings to fold,
But just that I might be kept near
The miracles I missed right here.

Let me learn how speckled scales
Can walk up waterfalls on silver tails,
And how the lithe snake sheds his skin
Yet never wears his brilliance thin.

And when I rest, as evening falls,
Let cock pheasants spread their paisley shawls
Upon me as the dappled fawn
Makes my pillow until dawn.

So much of heaven is close by
That I'll be happy here beneath the sky,
Since Paradise would promise less
Away from this wild Holiness.

EVENING DRESS

I've watched the swallows with their blue-steel shears
Picot the bias edge of fraying sky.
I've seen the blackbirds baste their long black threads
And hem night into day as they flew by.

I've gazed while nighthawks cut the pattern out,
Pinning it bright with sequins stars have strewn;
And then, at last, the low-cut V of geese,
Trying their plunging neckline on the moon.

the people

DAUGHTER

She held her veil aside and reached to him
Whose hair had caught the snowstorm years ago,
And pressed her young lips warm against his cheek;
Her hands found his; she wanted him to know
How glad she was that he was also hers.
The ties she tied were not of blood or water,
But of the spirit, hungry through the years;
For he who raised all sons had now a daughter
He could not see, because of manly tears.

PUMP HANDLE

The hickory on the old pump split apart,
And Gramp allowed as how he'd make a fitter
Handle from a piece of maple heart,
To fetch a drink for thirsty man and critter.

For a maple has the know-how. It can draw
That sweetness from the secret-flavored well
As puts all other trees to say, "Oh pshaw!"
As though they'd do as much, to hear them tell.

We rigged the maple handle, Gramp and I,
And he took hold to test its swing and teeter;
Then pumped the tin cup full for me to try,
And Glory be; that water tasted sweeter!

THE RIDER

He was all cotton candy and Buffalo Bill;
The carousel stopped, but not quite still,
As the music blared from the calliope band
And a sharp dime burned in his sweaty hand.

He was sheriff and posse and rustler too,
But the crowd pushed past as crowds will do;
As he made for the horse of his own delight
The impatient pony moved on out of sight.

He'd be darned if he'd ride on a duck or a pig,
Or sit on the seat of a chariot-rig;
He needed a saddle, a steed of his own,
So he stood as he rode, and he stood alone.

Now, when he comes to that merry-go-round,
He runs past the ponies because he has found
That he holds the new reins of rhythm and rhyme
And rides a wild zebra into Time.

THE TURNING

She was all T-shirt and faded blue jeans,
With a hit, and a run, and a slide to the base;
Pink gummy bubbles ballooned from her tongue,
It was snap—crack—and go-wash-your-face.

Her toes-all-out sneakers were first to the tree.
With a hide—seek—ready-or-not;
Follow the leader, and walk on the fence,
It was climb—jump—land-on-this-spot.

Then something happened to make her all girl.
With a blouse—skirt—and a what-keeps-it-up?
But the part that was boy has turned wistfully sad,
With a kick—scuff—and a come-along-pup.

ALL LOVELINESS

While sunbeams tiptoed through your hair
Weaving it soft and sunny,
The bee came to your petaled mouth
And left it strewn with honey.

The bunting's wing that brushed your eye
Gave blue forever after,
And my dumb voice has learned to sing
Because I heard your laughter.

The white birch laid its gracefulness
Upon your form and motion,
All loveliness has waited on
You, out of blithe devotion.

So now your pulsing heart has caught
My own and holds it raptured;
Yet never has it beat so free
As I behold it, captured.

YOU LEAVE SPRINGS OF APRILS

Take the summer with its lovely lakes,
The swirling wheat in the wind-wakes;
Then, though the mower comes to mow,
You leave springs of Aprils as you go.

Take the autumn with brooks now mellowed,
Leaf-dappled, willow-yellowed—
The goblet-grapes upon the vine
Where bittersweet and woodbine twine;
Yet, when there's nothing more to flow,
You leave springs of Aprils as you go.

Take the winter with ponds in panes,
And all north-pointing weathervanes;
Though I am drifted in ice and snow,
You leave springs of Aprils as you go.

IN THE KEY OF "C"

These are the things I like in "C":
Cathedrals and cottages
And cardinals in a cedar tree.
    Cream from a dairy
    Seed catalogues in January
    And courtesies that are customary.
I like cadets in cadence
Men's choirs and campfires
And cameos in candlelight;
    Camellias in a girl's dark hair
    Calypso and Camelot
    And a small cafe *sur le mer,*
A collie on a calendar
And small things that curl
Like a baby with its fist a-furl;
    And carnations in my coat lapel,
    Cake, three tiered—and chocolate,
    And children on a carousel;
Chorales and concerts in duet.
Corps de ballet, crystal chandeliers
And cadenzas by a cool clarinet.

Chicken cacciatore, Cheddar cheese,
Corn on the cob, cardamom and caraway
And a sticky bun savoring of cinnamon.
    I like commencements, color guards,
    Carillons in campus towers
    And the small cry in "good-bye."
Cupid, couples, and courtships,
Corsages, confetti and all the rest
And next year a christening with a cherub blessed.
    And Chinese lanterns and blue Nankin
    Ch'ing carvings, wind chimes,
    Rice cakes and a bamboo screen.
I like Christmas carols and candy canes
Chimneys and chestnuts
And icicles at the window panes;
    Oh, I like things that begin with "C,"
    But most of all, and dear to me,
    Are the C's I see in CECILY.

LONELY HEARTH

The off-key wind is whistling through its teeth
While strings are tuned by pizzicato rain;
The bare bough scrapes against my lonesome room,
Rapping its knuckles on my windowpane.

My winter's hearth is losing summer's glow,
I'll make some coffee, pour a cup of cheer,
Play records . . . read a book—it is no use,
The fingering chill comes on . . . and you not here.

MEMORY: HAVING AT ONE'S FINGER TIPS

He said that violets were out of time
And sold me a camellia for her hair—
She found a bobby pin and fixed it there.

We walked the aisles and visited Van Gogh,
She posed for Rembrandt in a pantomime;
We had a picnic—never spent a dime.

Yet, how the coin of that dear day has worn
Golden and warm and oh, so sweetly slow,
Till memory is all I have to show.

Now, when I hold this flower in my hand,
Remembering again that summer morn,
I flinch—and find camellias hide a thorn.

LOVE IS FOUR INITIALS

I returned to my schoolhouse of long years ago,
The latch to the entry was stopped with a nail;
It protested my hand, yet the door opened slow,
And my heart skipped a beat—my cheek became pale

For there at each desk was a face that I knew:
There was Maisie and Marjory, Roger and Roy;
Cowlicks and pigtails sitting close, two by two,
One berry-lipped girl to one sunburned boy.

I walked through the misting of love and of chalk
And found my old seat, the third from the end;
(The shy, girlish giggles, the swaggering talk)
Their faces were lovely, not one but a friend.
I sat at my place though the desk had grown small,
My fingers traced over the time-tempered wood,
And there as I knew, by memory's recall,
Found carved the four letters that only they could.

I lifted my head and called to her there,
But the room had come empty, my schoolmates had gone
Barefooted, beribboned, in September's air,
Leaving me with the initials I'd drawn.

My heart had not held her, nor had she kept mine,
The tremble of young love is a trying of wings;
Still the record is there on that old desk of pine
And the pulse won't forget the flutter it brings.

SHAPE OF A RING

Rings have such lovely shape;
The things they hold will not escape.
Circles of love that comprehend
No beginning . . . and no end.

This she gave to her oldest one:
A band of gold with a piece of sun
Caught in the topaz on its rim—
November's gem belonged to him.

IF, IN THE YEARS AHEAD

If, in the years ahead, you stand alone,
Whisper my name, and I'll come to your side,
And all those golden memories we own
Will press about you in their tender tide.
Within the lonely exile of your heart,
I'll come with love as I have always done,
No solitudes of life can ever part
Us from the warming of our true love's sun.
I'll hold you in the cling of my embrace,
You'll know my kiss, roughhewn as walnut bark,
Yet sweet as tamarind on lip and face;
The light will come, and there'll be no more dark.
  Closer than breath or sight or touch, I'll stay—
  Believe, my love, I'll not be far away.

THE WOMAN TAKEN

"Ho! Rabbi, standing there—
See what we caught in our snare."
A clutter of men in the marketplace
Came dragging a woman by her arms and hair.
   They closed and opened like a fang-filled face,
   Then, with a shout, spat her out
   To huddle at the Rabbi's feet
   Clutching the shroud of her guilty sheet.

Her accusers ran to the ruined wall
And broke off fragments until they all
Held in their fists the verdict stone
As she lay crumpled and alone.

The Rabbi spoke above the din,
"This woman's guilt is some man's sin.
How then can any stone you cast
Condemn the first but not the last?"

"Ho! Rabbi, standing there—
The law is just; the law is fair.
Take a stone in your holy hand
And strike with us who so declare."
    But He stood away from the righteous band
    And on his knee kneeled to see
    The travesty they never saw:
    The woman, broken, on the broken law.

THE MANY SHAPES OF CROSSES

There are many shapes of crosses
Other than the timbered "T";
I have seen men stitched on barb wire
Like a scarecrow effigy.

Men have wept upon long tables,
Heads on hands, with elbows spread,
Crucified by man's injustice,
Not quite living—not quite dead.

Others stand on high horizons,
Arms flung out in wide embrace,
Loving their fellowmen while knowing
Some will drive the spikes in place.

Wooden crosses kill more quickly
The body that is there impaled,
While others walk as human crosses
On which the heart alone is nailed.

Let the Crucifixion answer
Even now as it did then;
May we learn the shape of justice,
And not make crosses out of men.

BEAUTY IS HOW DEEP?

His was a pocked and pug-ugly mug,
Enough to make Lon Chaney shudder,
Or Bull Montana grin at last,
Or Tugboat Annie turn her rudder.

His face not only would stop a clock,
It would make an hourglass back up,
But he would fix our broken bikes,
And help us find our home-lost pup.

He ate his scabby harvest apples—
The perfect ones were ours to keep.
The best he had he gave to others;
His homeliness was just skin deep.

PRAYER AT EAST DOVER

He bows in the pulpit and offers the prayer;
We lean in the pews and listen with care.
The school for diviners has made him respect
The rules and the forms, and his prayer is correct:
    "O Thou Eternal, Almighty Being,
    All-powerful, All-wise, All-knowing, All-seeing,
    Omniscient Author, Creator, and Cause,
    Deity, Godhead, and Giver of Laws
    Lay on the parishioners of this parish
    Thy promised blessings they so cherish,
    Go with those who travel today
    And see them safely along their way,
    Keep us all in the best of health
    And give us our share of labor's wealth. . . ."
The pastor stops, and I glance to see
What is upsetting him in his plea;

He knows too well and sets it right,
Bringing particulars into our sight:
"Dear Father, please help Mrs. Johnson to breathe,
These foggy days make her tired lungs heave,
Move out the mist and lighten the air
And give her the ease of her rocking chair.
Take the bruised hurt out of young Nathan's arm;
It aches him so when he's haying the farm."
Anonymous people, too vague, too broad,
Are not so effective, petitioned to God
Who less to the public, again and again
Bends more to the person, amen, amen!

THE CONSTANT THIRST

I watched her scuff along the village street,
Her one-button coat was brown, and wind-thin;
And muddied stockings sloughed above her feet.
Stiff wisps of hair stuck out from what had been
A kerchief of flowers, when it was new.
But finger smudge and soot had blotted out
What charm had been in either of the two.
Her mouth chewed silent words—but what about?
Then, like a golden leaf in sun-splashed tree,
A yellow warbler sang into the skies,
Giving back to the sun such melody
The old one stopped—and raised her winter eyes.
   Bubbles of song, bursting from April's cup
    Spilled down on her. She drank. And hope looked up.

PORTRAIT AMONG THE PERENNIALS

Though autumn's colors run flagrantly,
Flamboyant with each newcomer,
Blue chicory and Queen Anne's lace
Are the loveliest leftovers of summer.

And once I saw in a Sunday crowd,
Amid its stained-glass color,
A weed of a woman in white and blue
That made all the rest look duller.

A wispy, dusty white she was—
—blue hat—and a cane of hickory;
I see her every time I see
Queen Anne's lace and chicory.

ON SECOND THOUGHT

The village dump is smoldering in the marsh;
I'm here with crates of trumperies and trash,
And yet disowning ownership is harsh
As these are flung to smithereen and smash.
This footstool, bid at auction for small cash,
I toss upon the ritualistic pyre;
Though something in me burns and turns to ash
Whenever I discard what I admire.
And so it is when each long-lived desire
Of its own weight assuredly will crash
As going, going, gone into the fire
Remorse flares up and feeds the final flash.
    It's then my neighbors' junk, of which they tire,
    Excites in me a new need to acquire.

THREE FOR A DOLLAR

I wandered through the book sale on the mall—
Loose in their spines old novels slumped among
the biblios, biographies, and all
That spilled from racks, or to each other clung.
I passed translations, annotated tomes,
The how-to-do-it manuals (with chart),
And there beyond "Genetic Chromosomes"
Found Poetry as nearer to the heart.
Then suddenly—unwarned—indignant-smitten
I saw, mid shards of verse and Grecian urns,
The slender volume I myself had written,
Between the works of Shakespeare and of Burns.
   Chagrined at first—the day was saved for me:
   I've never been in better company.

WINTER MILKING

Above his barn all diamond-crusted,
Stars and moon were sugar-dusted.
A thousand mice squeaked under foot
As he went stomping out and put
His one brown milker through the doors
That shut out winter from his chores.

He climbed the mow above the dairy
And brought June down to February,
Then found his stool and went to her,
His tiger cat began to purr.
He bent, and took the steamy milk
That whispered softly as white silk.
The barn eaves shivered in the gale;
His thighs grew warm around the pail,
And he felt good, and far from sin,
With zero out and his cow in.

SIDE HILL FARMER

His life was uphill like his haying,
With hardship and ill fortune preying
Parasitic on their host,
He never had much chance to coast.

Yet up he climbed and kept on trying
Till he grew too tired for dying—
Lay exhausted, could not make
The final step he had to take.

Above the valley's pointing spire,
His native hills stood steeples higher
Where God leaned down to fourscore seven,
And gave a hand-up into heaven.

A LIKING FOR WOODEN THINGS

My uncle liked to work with wood,
And I did too, as his nephew should.
His love for wood was never fickle;
By George! He'd take a wooden nickel,
Insisting it was worth far more
Than something hammered out of ore.
His pitchfork, cut from a hickory tree
Was already tined where it branched to three.
Worn in the handle of his maul
I find his hands, and I recall
The log he adzed out for his cattle's
Watering trough. It had no rattles
As the galvanized tank his neighbors bought.
His axebit knew just what it ought
To make the grain come smooth to touch.
Some say that doesn't amount to much
And ask where bridges would be today
If it weren't for steel to hold the way?

And I agree, but keep my thanks
For the backroad bridge with wooden planks.
My uncle had the feel that brings
A liking for all wooden things.
I hope my hand will hold as well
The words I've often heard him tell:
Wood will fit itself to man
More than iron ever can.

MY FATHER'S HOUSE

This cottage waited through my yearning years,
Patient for me and my hand on its latch;
My father's home, its gates like straining ears,
Waiting in England's isle of stone and thatch.

And then at last, with Time and ocean spanned,
Standing this day within its Kentish lane,
I saw his birthplace, felt the touch firsthand,
And wondered how my love could bear the pain.

I braved it out and walked up to the door,
Sensitive to its aged, enduring wood;
Though it was locked—there, where the lintel wore
I viewed what any son would see . . . or could,
   Then turned, composed, until I saw, too late,
   A poppy break its heart beside the gate.

CROSSROADS STORE

My country store of childhood is no more,
Its shelves are bare, the lock is on the door.
I press my face against the clouded glass
As through its dusty lenses old years pass.
The grocer scoops brown sugar from the bin,
He winks at me and drops a hard lump in.
I watch him as he scores a pound of cheese,
His knife will not cut thin, more likely squeeze
A little past the weight, and in my favor.
The dark molasses barrel I can savor
With finger held against the spigot's drip,
Its heavy honey sticky on my lip.
Dimly I see where old men sat and wove
Legend, and myth, and fact around the stove.
Though breath of years has fogged the window scene,
Memory's sleeve has rubbed my eyesight clean.

LET'S HEAR IT FOR THE FOURTH OF JULY!

I got up early this Fourth of July,
Unfurled the flag and let it fly
Upright from its curbstone socket.
I missed the firecrackers,
The sky-sparkling rocket,
Remembering back when my small thumb
Was twice as big, was swollen numb
With black and blue and purple hues
From a piece of punk and a too-short fuse.
We're safer and saner I do not deny,
But I still miss the BANG! of that Fourth of July.

No bands in parade, no ballgames to play,
The uncommon date is a commonplace day;
No posters on barns announcing the circus,
No tug-of-war teams to pull us and jerk us—
Independence is silent, no concerts, no speeches,
We take from our country like bloodsucking leeches,
Yet never a hip-hip hooray or a cheer
For the bloodstream that brought us to this golden year.

The flag that we see in the dawn's early light,
Other hands raised in the dusk of the night.
Sometimes we have failed both the brave and the free,
Still the true patriot sees what his country can be.
That we're safer in silence, I do deny:
We should shout and go BANG! on the Fourth of July.

MOLASSES COOKIES

These cookies had a ways to go
Before this northern boy could know

That tongues can dance as well as feet,
When ginger and molasses meet.

All plump and hot from oven door,
And blessed with sugar . . . nothing more.

The songs he sings are of the south,
Louisiana's in his mouth!

It takes a good, long sugar cane
To pour molasses into Maine.

REACH TO THE ROSE

Life has this dilemma
that hooks us on its horns:
Is the thornbush full of roses,
or the rosebush full of thorns?

Whatever is the answer
that living may disclose,
though fingers flinch at bleeding
I'll still reach to the rose.

TRAILING ARBUTUS

Her head was always up among the stars;
She walked that way, stretching beyond her reach.
Her toes were bruised, her shins were notched with scars;
She watched the gulls but never knew the beach.

She climbed the tallest pine tree with her eyes
And marveled when she found the eagle's lair.
That tree so high! She could not realize
She stood upon the roots that kept it there.

But Time is wise and kinder than we know.
It would not let her go, nor would it cheat,
And so at last it bent her down to show
That all the while stars twinkled at her feet.

FIXED FOCUS

Her eyes were always fixed upon the ground,
She liked to know precisely where she stood;
No stone or hidden root but what she found
It first, and so removed the likelihood
That she would stumble, stub her toe, or slip.
And so she went her picky, cautious way,
Avoiding obstacles where she might trip,
Though one would hardly say her walk was gay.
She missed the clouds, the gull, the apple tree
Caught with its boughs a-bloom against the sky,
But she knew well just where her feet would be,
Yet neither sun nor stars shone in her eye.
　One never drains the fullness of the cup
　Until one learns to drink it looking up.

PILGRIMAGE TO THE GRAVE OF
ROBERT PETER TRISTRAM COFFIN

I found him dreaming on Cranberry Horn,
His gravestone crowding the country road;
Asleep in the land where his poems were born,
Lulled by the songs the sea-wind blowed.

It seemed so right that he chose to be
Right up close where he could see
His neighbors passing from Brunswick town
To Cundy's Harbor, farther down.

Spruce and wild strawberries living in stone!
(The green-boughed poet, his sweet red-love)
I kneeled and knew I was not alone,
Something of him was beneath and above.

I searched him out who called me friend,
And found his leaving was not the end;
I'd come with a tear and thoughts of death,
And left with a smile . . . and a deeper breath.

HE WAS MY TEACHER

He harrowed minds with curving question marks,
Teaching as much outside the book as in;
He'd listen out the window for Spring larks,
Postponing Euclid's chalky discipline.

He kept the burr of "Why?" beneath the tail
Of every sluggard slouched down in his seat,
Our spines came straight—we did not dare to fail,
And we survived by thinking on our feet.

He was my teacher—wise—yet hard as knots,
I tried to pick him loose and so undo him.
But he was miles ahead of all my plots:
I've found instead that he has tied me to him.

ONE STEP OF TRIUMPH

My feet shall never stand on Everest's peak,
Nor smudge the sands of undiscovered shore.
My ears shall never hear the waters roar
Where jungle rivers fall in Mozambique.
For me, no stratospheric flights; I seek
No depths uncharted to the ocean floor.
These will come to others who explore
The geographic goals of which they speak.
Still, I have known the high discovery,
Moments when exultation held my hand,
And these have come in no exotic land,
While just one step from my back porch will show
A world and year unsearched, that beckons me
To cast first print in New Year's printless snow.

"LET HIM DENY HIMSELF . . ."

This is my trial and tribulation, Lord:
Must I deny my Self to follow thee?
I want to be disciple, not a ward;
Do you not want the Self, the I, the Me?
For how am I to turn my back on Self?
Two fathers cast their image in my frame:
A lump of clay from one's celestial shelf,
The other gave me features and his name.
Let me be more than slight statistic in
The world's increasing census; let my face
Be mine that in the crowded, noisy din
My Self may be my own best dwelling place.

     Although your patience with me must be tried,
     I come to you as Self—not Self denied.

WHOSE ZOO?

Yes, there is one of everything in me:
The snail, the snake; the hummingbird, the crow.
Within my feet the hare moves cautiously,
While lions roar upon my heart's plateau.
The sluggish carp, scavenger of the mud,
Swims in my veins, and yet the fin-winged trout
With rainbows on his sides leaps through my blood,
Rising and falling, throbbing to be out.
For I am all these creatures in my time,
They take their turns at living in my skin;
I sense it when the jungle jaguars climb
Along my spine—I recognize these kin.
Never a dull day, living as I do—
Caretaker of this strangely private zoo.

SOMETHING HE KNOWS

Out of the dark, out of his unknown past,
Something he knows still haunts man's present fate;
Some memory of consciousness holds fast
The inkling of his dim and prior state.
What made him swim away from ocean salt,
Taking a manlike chance on gulping air;
Or having climbed the mangrove, risked the vault
From scale to wing—and dare a human dare?
Why does he take the gamble with such leaps,
Then, when he feels at home, home is no place
He knows? It's more his inner realm he keeps,
Kicking the earth away from outer space.
  Yet on he ventures, rides the rocket's ember,
  Still homesick for a home he can't remember.

REVERENCE

There in the dawning of my delight
I stood on tiptoe to the sky.
Sunflushed and dewcooled
I sipped the spill of day from the sun's
W-i-d-e-l-i-p-p-e-d-g-o-b-l-e-t.
    The wind was fingering the harp-edged leaves
    Where a grey squirrel signed himself
    Tail and all
    Into a silver treble clef.
    Young trout were dimpling the waters
    All crows were doves
    And every snake moved in love with the bright
      birds.
This was my Sabbath and I was priest and
  parishioner
Praying my hymns to the reedy marshes
And singing my prayers to the
  morning-mantled-mountains.
My feet stepped joyously among the sunfish
Where the fans of the sea were folding
And forever everlastingly unfolding.
The waters opened and took me in.
I became seal, serpent, and Poseidon

Domiciled in the dominion of the waves.
I eased apart their blue transparencies
Flinging skyward pearls of light
From my fingers dripping.
    While, at a little way, a muskrat
    Climbed up a submerged stump
    Where he rested, holding a prayer
    In his front paws.
It was then I turned, and could have, had I willed
Walked upon the lake, not by faith, but
By exultation—
        so worshipful I was.
I reached the shore, stood tall
And raising my arms palms-up
Offered Him such glory as I knew.
    I was Adam before the fall.

WILD AND HOLY RAGE

He stood before the old, abandoned barn
Where grass had taken over doorbar deep,
Warming the winding tunnels with its yarn
Where woodchucks burrow in for winter's keep.
The beams were sprung, the rafters' backs were broken,
The shingles softened with the mossy stain,
And there his eye caught up the barn's best token:
The running stallion on the weathervane.
Through the deep night he runs his starlit course,
And into day outruns the transient wind;
The heart vaults up and rides this leaping horse,
The robust will comes back that life had thinned.
   Over the tired and ruined limbs of age
   The spirit runs, in wild and holy rage.